LITTLE LIBRARY

Horses

Christopher Maynard

Kingfisher Books

NEW YORK

Contents

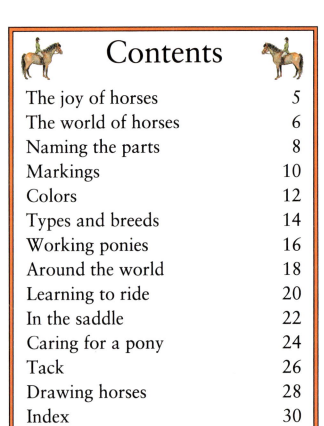

The joy of horses

A galloping horse with its flowing mane and tail is a sight that people never forget. For those who love horses and ponies their strength and speed is often part of the attraction.

Today, many people go riding just for fun and for the exercise, and some also take part in competitions. If they have their own horse, all the hard work, care, and attention are worth it when they saddle up and ride off.

The world of horses

There are about 300 kinds, or breeds, of horses and ponies and they come in many sizes and colors.

Some horses are bred to gallop quickly in races, while others have to be strong so they can pull heavy loads. Ponies like the Icelandic or Shetland are tough and are used to cold, northern winters.

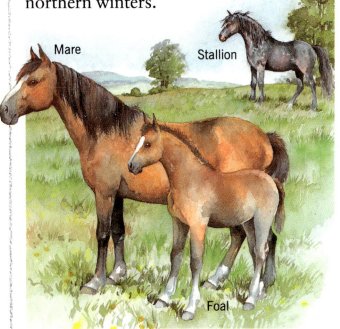

Mare

Stallion

Foal

Icelandic pony

Shetland pony

△ Horses that measure less than 14 hands are called ponies. A fully grown Shetland pony is about 10 hands, and an Icelandic pony is 12 to 13 hands.

Ponies are usually gentle and sensible so they are a good choice for someone who is learning to ride.

◁ A baby horse is called a foal. At the age of one it becomes a yearling. Its mother is called a mare and its father a stallion.

HOW HIGH?

A horse's height is measured in hands from the ground up to the top of its withers. Each hand is 4 inches (10 cm) high.

Naming the parts

The different parts of a horse are called points, and all horses have the same ones whatever breed they are. Each point has a special name.

Together, the points of a horse make up its confirmation. If a horse has good confirmation, all its parts are the right size and shape.

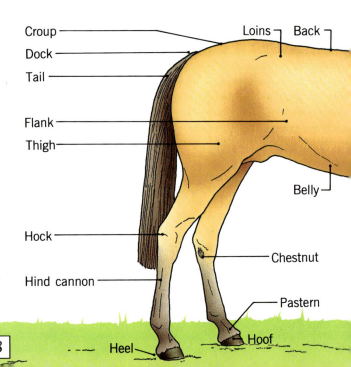

Croup

Dock

Tail

Flank

Thigh

Hock

Hind cannon

Loins

Back

Belly

Chestnut

Pastern

Hoof

Heel

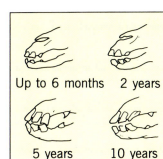

Up to 6 months　　2 years

5 years　　10 years

Teeth show a pony's age. Baby teeth appear soon after birth. By 5 years, a pony has a full set. As it gets older, its teeth get longer.

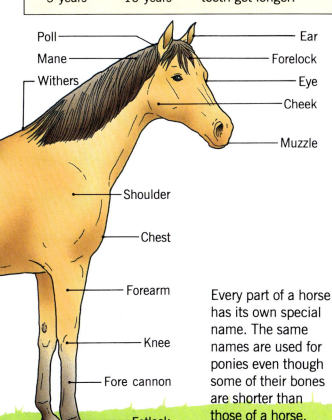

Poll — Ear

Mane — Forelock

Withers — Eye

— Cheek

— Muzzle

— Shoulder

— Chest

— Forearm

— Knee

— Fore cannon

— Fetlock

Every part of a horse has its own special name. The same names are used for ponies even though some of their bones are shorter than those of a horse.

9

Markings

Many horses have marks on their heads, legs, and bodies. These have special names. Any mark on the forehead, for example, is a "star", even if it is not exactly star-shaped.

Star

Race

Blaze

Snip

White face

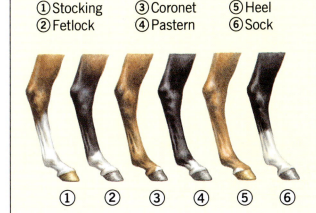

LEG MARKINGS

The markings on a horse's legs have different names. A white marking that goes all the way up the leg is a "full stocking." If it only reaches the knee it is a "stocking."

① Stocking   ③ Coronet   ⑤ Heel
② Fetlock   ④ Pastern   ⑥ Sock

①   ②   ③   ④   ⑤   ⑥

A "race" is the name for a white line down the center of a horse's face, while a long, wide, white band is a "blaze." If the white band spreads out to the eyes it is called a "white face." A small white mark on the muzzle is a "snip."

A white patch on the body is just called a "white patch." A horse with no markings at all is "whole-colored."

Colors

Horses come in many different colors. The five main ones are black, brown, bay, chestnut, and dun.

1 Chestnuts are red-brown, and roans have white hairs in their coat.

2 Piebalds have big black and white patches. Skewbalds are brown and white. Cream is a rare color.

3 Brown horses are brown all over. Duns are sandy with black manes and tails, and palominos have a golden coat and a silvery mane and tail.

4 Black horses are black all over. Grays have black and white hairs in their coat, and bays are brown with black manes, tails, and legs.

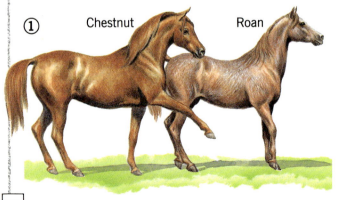

①   Chestnut   Roan

② Piebald   Skewbald

Cream

③ Brown   Dun   Palomino

④ Black   Gray   Bay

13

Types and breeds

Horses are divided into types. Their type depends on how they are used, and their breed. Carthorses and polo ponies are two different types. Shire horses, Friesians, and Arabs are all different breeds.

▷ Percherons were first bred in France. They are a type of draft horse. Draft horses are the largest and strongest horses.

Percheron

Shire

Friesian

◁ At 19 hands, the Shire horse is the tallest breed of all the draft horses.

◁ Long ago, Friesian draft horses were used by heavily armored knights to ride into battle.

Thoroughbred   Arab   Morgan

△ Thoroughbreds are used for racing. They have all been bred from just three Arab stallions.

△ Arabs are one of the oldest breeds in the world. The Morgan is a popular family horse.

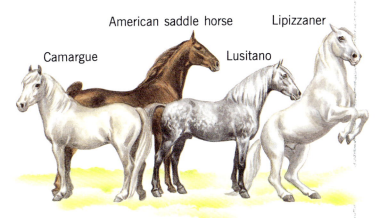

American saddle horse   Lipizzaner

Camargue   Lusitano

△ Camargue horses live in wild herds in southern France. The American saddle horse is a show ring horse.

△ The Lusitano is known for its bravery in bull rings. Lipizzaners learn clever tricks at a riding school in Vienna.

15

Working ponies

Ponies are amazingly strong and hardy, in spite of their small size. For this reason they are used as working animals in many countries. In the mountains of Austria, for example, Haflinger ponies often have the job of pulling loaded sleds in snowy weather.

Criollo

Haflinger

△ Tough Criollo ponies are ridden by cowboys in South America.

△ The Haflinger stands 14 hands tall. It may be chestnut or palomino.

Fjording

Welsh Cob

Shetland

The Fjording is a Norwegian dun pony. It is used on mountain farms instead of a tractor. Welsh Cobs are strong. They are used for pulling carts.

Over a hundred years ago the Shetland was used in the coal mines of northern England.

Other ponies include the Sumba which can be trained to dance. The Hocaido is known for its speed, and the piebald Pinto was bred by Native Americans as a war horse. The Pony of the Americas is a young person's pony.

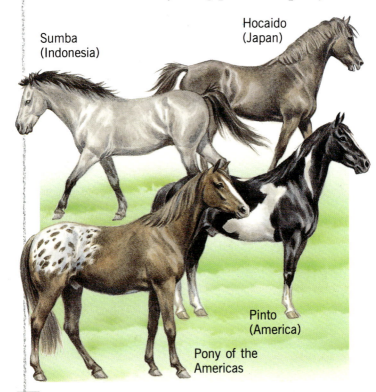

Sumba
(Indonesia)

Hocaido
(Japan)

Pinto
(America)

Pony of the
Americas

Start a scrapbook on horses and ponies. Try drawing your own pictures, or cut them out of magazines. List all the things you can find out about each type of horse.

▷ The Falabella is the smallest pony in the world. It is less than 7 hands high, about the size of a big dog, but over a short distance it can gallop faster than a racehorse. Falabellas come from Argentina. They used to be bred as pets and are not used for riding, but sometimes pull small carts.

Learning to ride

If you want to learn to ride, the best way is to join a riding school. It's a good idea to visit the stables first, before you start taking lessons.

On your visit you can look at the ponies, talk to the riding teacher, and watch a lesson in action so that you know what to expect when you start.

A hard, well-fitting riding hat is very important.

A short, waterproof jacket will keep out wind and rain.

Corduroy trousers are better than jeans, which can rub your knees.

Wear boots or walking shoes with a small, flat heel.

Clothes for riding should fit comfortably.

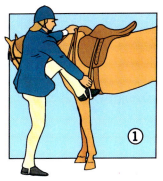

1 To mount, stand on the pony's left side with the reins in your left hand. Lift your left foot into the stirrup, holding the stirrup steady with your right hand.

2 Put your right hand on the saddle and spring up. Then swing your right leg over the pony's back.

Once you have learned how to control your pony, you may be taken out into the countryside. This kind of riding is called hacking. But if you have to ride along any roads, stay in single file and well out of the way of any cars.

In the saddle

S itting correctly in the saddle is very important. You should sit in the deepest part of the saddle. Keep your back straight, shoulders back, and head up. Try not to lean forward.

You can practice the correct way to hold the reins at home using two chairs and some string. Tie the string to one chair and sit astride the second chair. Hold the reins as shown.

Horses move at four different paces. The walk has four hoof beats as each hoof hits the ground in turn. The trot has two beats, the canter three, and the gallop four beats.

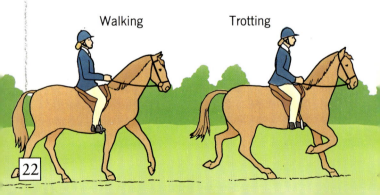

Walking

Trotting

Hold the inside of your thighs against the saddle, but don't grip too tightly or you'll get sore legs. You should make sure you keep the reins low, close to the pony's neck.

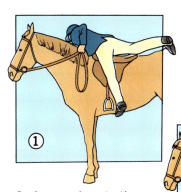

1 To dismount, take both feet out of the stirrups. Then swing your right leg over the pony's back.

2 As you drop to the ground on the pony's left side, you should end up facing the saddle. Make sure you keep hold of the reins.

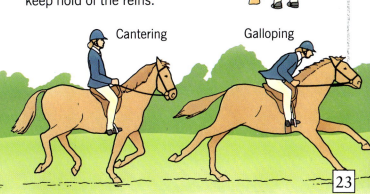

Cantering

Galloping

Caring for a pony

L ooking after a pony is hard work. A pony that lives in a stable needs to have fresh water, food, and exercise every single day of the year. Cleaning the stable thoroughly must be done each day as well.

A pony kept in a field needs a good supply of fresh water, and somewhere to shelter. It should be checked every day to make sure it hasn't hurt itself.

A pony in a box stall needs lots of hay and regular feeds of grain and bran. The stall or stable should be cleaned out every day and fresh straw put on the floor.

These brushes are used for grooming a pony. The metal pick is for cleaning mud out of hooves. The currycomb is used for cleaning the horse's coat.

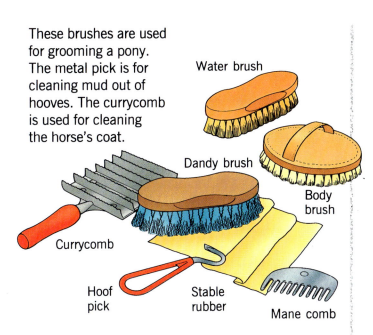

Water brush

Dandy brush

Body brush

Currycomb

Hoof pick

Stable rubber

Mane comb

An outdoor pony should be groomed less than a pony in a stable. It needs to keep the grease in its coat to stay warm and dry.

Tack

S addles, bridles, and the other pieces of equipment needed for riding are all known as tack. Straps and buckles are used to adjust the bridle and saddle so the pony and you feel comfortable when you set off. With practice you will learn to know how the tack should feel and be able to adjust it yourself.

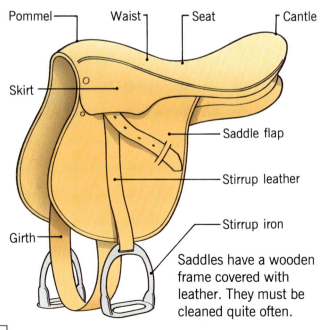

Pommel — Waist — Seat — Cantle

Skirt —

Saddle flap

Stirrup leather

Stirrup iron

Girth —

Saddles have a wooden frame covered with leather. They must be cleaned quite often.

The bridle is a leather harness which slips over the horse's head. The reins are attached to the bit – a metal or rubber bar that fits inside the horse's mouth.

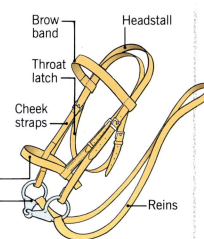

Brow band

Headstall

Throat latch

Cheek straps

Nose band

Snaffle bit

Reins

1 When you are ready to put on the bridle, slip the reins carefully over the horse's head so that they lie on the neck.

2 Hold the headstall, and put the horse's nose through the nose band. Carefully guide the bit into its mouth.

3 Slip the headstall over the ears. Check the brow band sits well. Buckle the throat latch to hold it all in place.

Drawing horses

It isn't difficult to draw a horse. If you follow the steps shown here, you will soon learn how to do it.

The secret is to start with the basic shapes first, then fill in the details at the very end.

A STANDING HORSE

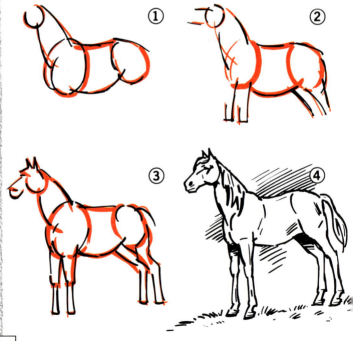

A HORSE'S HEAD

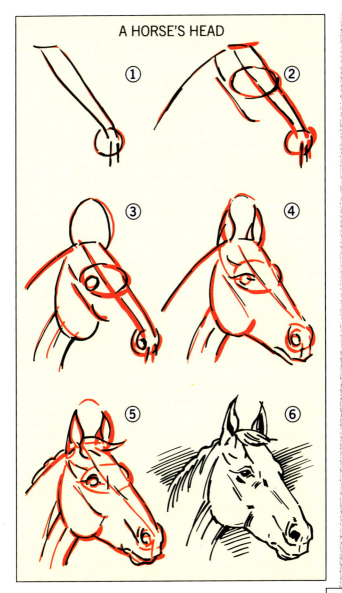

Index